The Invisible War

A Glimpse Into Spiritual Warfare

Written by
Velma J. Colston Biggers

"My people are destroyed for lack of knowledge..."
— Hosea 4:6
"...but through knowledge shall the just be delivered." —
Proverbs 11:9
"And ye shall know the truth, and the truth shall make you
free." — John 8:32

The Invisible War: A Glimpse Into Spiritual Warfare
Copyright © 2022 by Velma J. Colston Biggers

ISBN: 9798351329314
Published by Habakkuk Publishing
Location: Southfield
Edited by Naomi Books, LLC
Printed in the United States of America

Disclaimer

Although the author has made every effort to ensure that the information in this book was correct at press time and while this publication is designed to provide accurate information in regard to the subject matter covered, the author/publisher assumes no responsibility for errors, inaccuracies, omissions, or any other inconsistencies herein and hereby disclaim any liability to any party for any loss, damage, or disruption caused by errors or omissions, whether such errors or omissions result from negligence, accident or any other cause. This publication is meant as a source of valuable information for the reader, however, it is not meant as a substitute for direct expert assistance. If such level of assistance is required, the services of an expert professional should be sought.

Table of Contents

TABLE OF CONTENTS

Foreword

*In her outstanding new book, **The Invisible War- A Glimpse Into Spiritual Warfare**, Pastor Biggers biblically informs and strategizes how we can stop living lives that are dislodged, dismayed, and destroyed by the invisibility and incorporeality of Satan's shenanigans. In her divine wisdom, Pastor Biggers understands that battles are not wars. and that there comes a time when we must cease battling and start warring against the diabolical forces that come to deny us our God-given destiny and purpose. Pastor Biggers and her anointed book can convince all who read that you can live victoriously and exist righteously when you fight effectively and profoundly according to the Word of God.*

Dr. Charles Graham Jr. PhD, LMSW, MA,
Divine Destiny Missions

Foreword by Apostle Nataki Tompkins

I am truly appreciative for The Invisible War written by Pastor Velma Biggers during this age of warfare that is happening within our society and homes naturally and spiritually. Now more than ever, believers in Christ Jesus need clarity understanding of this topic and how to fight with wisdom, maturity, and confidence. In this book, readers are given practical ways on how to build one's faith along with biblical strategies to destroy the Adversary's schemes individually and corporately that will give us the victory Christ spoke of. Pastor Biggers has been and remains to be a wealth of knowledge for many including myself through her years of experience in ministry in addition to the wisdom gained from personal encounters. Years ago, a well-known preacher made the statement "the potency of the anointing comes with age". I am a true believer of this and believe our elders need to be more revered than they are in this day and age. Therefore, soak up the wisdom from these pages that have been written for our benefit.

Love Broke The Chains Ministry

It is a privilege to know Pastor Velma Biggers. She is my sister in the Lord, my friend and a true servant of God. I strongly encourage the reading of *The Invisible War-A Glimpse Into Spiritual War-fare.* This book deals with the reality of spiritual warfare. It is very important for God's people to be able to determine when spiritual warfare is being engaged against us so that we can address it properly. This book gives great insight of what spiritual warfare looks like and how we should address it. As Believers, we must be able to discern the works of darkness opposed to natural life experiences. Well done, Pastor Biggers.

May God continue to strengthen you as you go forward in God's plan of salvation to many.

Apostle Dr. Vicki Byrd
Reformation Life Center Church International

Dedication

I dedicate this book to my loving husband of fifty years and partner for life, Minister Joseph Biggers, Sr., who encouraged me every step of the way. I could not have done this without his patience and coaching. To my children Joseph Jr., Nekhia and Landon Biggers who taught me to love unconditionally.

Most of all, I thank the Lord Jesus Christ, who entrusted me with this assignment and who continues to increase my knowledge and understanding of spiritual matters.

Father, I love you more than life!

Preface

I would like to begin by noting there are testimonials in this writing that may be alarming to some. If I did not have these experiences, like some of you, I might have some reservations believing the spirit realm exists and impacts the world on the level it does. However, contrary to what some of us have been taught, the spirit realm is as real as the physical world we live in today. There is activity occurring all around us. It is in the spirit realm that the children of God, as representatives of Christ, are called to war for the souls of men. Ephesians 6:12 makes it clear that our warfare is not fought in this world, but in a different realm. "For we wrestle not against flesh and blood, but against principalities, against powers, against the rulers of the darkness of this world, against spiritual wickedness in high places." (The Holy Bible, King James Version; all subsequent citations are from this version, unless otherwise noted.)

I will share things that God has revealed to me in the spirit realm. I write to encourage believers in Christ; not to promote fear, but to conquer it. II Timothy 1:7 states, "For God hath not given us the spirit of fear; but of power, and of love, and of a sound mind." I am also reminded and encouraged by what Jesus said to Simon Peter in Luke 22:32, which reads, "But I have prayed for thee, that thy faith fail not: and when thou art converted, strengthen thy brethren." It took me a long time to realize that my fight is not against flesh and blood, but with the spiritual source that may work through a person. An evil spirit needs a counterpart, a body, in order to be effective in its evil purpose. The person being used may not even be aware they are being influenced by a spirit. It is my prayer that those reading this book will become more aware of *The Invisible War* raging all around us, so we become more conscience of our purpose in the earth. I believe it is the responsibility of every believer of the Gospel of Jesus Christ to encourage and strengthen others, even as Christ has strengthened us.

Velma J. Colston Biggers

That we henceforth be no more children, tossed to and fro, and carried about with every wind of doctrine, by the sleight of men, and cunning craftiness, whereby they lie in wait to deceive; but speaking the truth in love, may grow up into him in all things, which is the head, even Christ:

— Ephesians 4:14-15

My Prayer for You

Father, in the Name of Jesus, I pray for those who read this book, that Your Spirit of Truth will minister to them. I pray this book will inspire them to search Your Word, and in doing so, cause them to fall deeper in love with You. I pray Your Word and this book will enlighten them and remove the scales from their eyes.

Father, bless them to find comfort and strength in that secret place in You, and to find Your divine purpose for their lives. Teach them to walk confidently in the anointing You have placed upon them. Bless them to prosper in all You have given them to do as they grow from children to sons of God.

Introduction

Did you hear that? Did you see that? No, you cannot hear it with your natural ear, nor see it with the natural eye, because it is occurring in the invisible realm of the spirit. Brethren, there is an invisible war raging all around us! It is a war between the Kingdom of Light and the Kingdom of Darkness — good versus evil competing for the souls of men. When I first witnessed this, I was at the altar in prayer. Suddenly, I could hear the sounds of warfare! I heard swords clinking and the loud voices of opposing forces in war. The location of this battleground was in the spirit realm. It was a place without color. I could not make out the forms of those in battle, but I knew it was intense! For a moment, the Lord allowed me to get a glimpse of *The Invisible War*!

"And from the days of John the Baptist until now the kingdom of heaven suffereth violence, and the violent take it by force."

— Matthew 11:12

Chapter One

My Introduction to the Spirit Realm

When I was 23 years old, I had my first wake-up call to an awareness of the spirit realm. I had fallen asleep in my bed with the lights on while reading a book. At the time, I was the mother of a young infant and a toddler. My husband worked the midnight shift. Somewhere in the early hours of the morning, approximately three o'clock, this overwhelming feeling of being suffocated awoke me from a peaceful sleep! It felt as if I was being enveloped in something that was overcoming me to the point it was literally cutting off my breath. I had stopped breathing when I heard a voice say, "Open your eyes." Immediately, I opened my eyes, and I saw a gray mist pulling away from me and moving out the door of my bedroom. It passed quickly, as if being pursued!

As I continued to lay there, confused and wondering what had just happened, I felt a tremendous presence of love engulf me. Trying to make sense of it, I reasoned that my departed brother had come back from the grave to visit me. It was the most wonderful and powerful feeling of love I had ever experienced! I did not want this presence to lift, but it did. All I knew for sure, is that something or someone loved me very much and had come to my rescue. I learned later that the enemy had come to take my life before my time, by premature death, but God said, "No!" The wonderful presence I had experienced was from God. They were ministering angels. While I did not understand all the specifics, I knew that when the presence of Light came, darkness had to flee! Now I know, without a doubt, it was not a loved one from the grave, because Ecclesiastes 9:56 implies that the dead have nothing to do with the living. People *do not* come back from the grave!

Why did God allow this experience? I now believe this was part of my introduction to the spirit realm. I had heard about young people in good health, dying in their sleep for no apparent reason. One such young lady I knew was approximately 21 years old. After my experience, it made sense. My main point of sharing this story is that there is a war going on, in the spirit, all around us, and we can no longer afford to remain ignorant.

In my thirties, I was no longer satisfied with the "norm" in church, and I began searching for the "more" I knew existed, because my spirit man craved it. I did not know how to explain it except to say I needed more than what my regular church attendance afforded me. I was no longer satisfied with milk as described in the Bible. 1 Corinthians 3:2 reads, "I gave you milk, not solid food, for you were not yet ready for it..." — The Holy Bible, New International Version (NIV). But I knew I was ready for more in my walk with God. As I became desperate to satisfy that feeling of hunger and void, I left my traditional church in search of what I later understood to be a deeper truth in Christ.

One winter evening, exhausted and frustrated with this unexplainable void, I got on my knees and cried out to the Lord, "I want to know the truth!" Yes, I knew partial truth. I knew Jesus was Lord, but my heart cried out to know so much more about Him! I could not have prayed this way if the Holy Spirit had not prompted me. "For it is God which worketh in you both to will and to do of his good pleasure." — Philippians 2:13. I knew I was tapping into something much bigger than I could ever imagine and there was no going back, because such knowledge would change the course of my life forever. Soon thereafter, God answered my prayer and sent a young woman to witness to me about a deeper truth and the awesome power of the Holy Spirit.

As a result of what the young woman shared with me and my family, the Holy Spirit led us to attend Maranatha Apostolic Ministries, a small church on the corner in the inner city. It was the type of church we used to think was peculiar, where they spoke in "tongues." It was in this small church that I met the love of my life, the Holy Spirit. I became one of those peculiar people, baptized in the Name of Jesus, dancing, singing, and speaking in tongues! It was here that I was first introduced to spiritual warfare. This small church moved in the power of deliverance and inner healing ministries, which I will discuss later. It was here that I witnessed and learned the basics of how to engage in spiritual warfare.

Young in the Lord, my husband and I would sit with our pastors as they ministered to the saints of God. These sessions were often one-on-one and lasted for hours. I learned how to listen for the Holy Spirit, and I learned about the discerning of spirits. I watched as they ministered to souls through what is called "the word of knowledge." I saw and heard demons' resistance to being evicted (cast out of people they were inhabiting) by the people of God. The pastors and ministers confidently pursued them until they gave up and left the person in whom they had taken residence.

I began to understand there was indeed a war going on all around us that involved good versus evil, and the victory was monumental, because the battle was for the souls of men! The revelation

I received from such teaching and experience is priceless. We witnessed many souls receive liberty from demonic oppression; many of these people were not even aware of the demonic presence! Later, I was very surprised to find out that the deliverance and inner healing ministries are foreign, and even rejected, in some spirit-filled churches! I believe it is due to the lack of knowledge of spiritual warfare and unfortunately, our enemy, Satan, and the demonic host rejoice over this.

Chapter Two

The Spirit Realm

Although we live in the natural realm of the flesh: touch, taste, sight, smell and hearing — there is another realm that co-exists with the natural — it is the spirit realm. For years, I would get glimpses of this realm. Like many people, I did not understand what I was seeing at first. However, I knew it was real because I was wide awake and alert (most of the time) when I saw into it. I did not search for it, though. At certain times, it was as if God would pull back the curtain and allow me to get a glimpse into what seemed like another dimension. I sensed it wasn't a normal experience. For fear some would think I had "lost it," I did not discuss it with anyone. When I was born again, however, I gained greater understanding that there was indeed another world with activity happening all around us. This is the spirit realm.

Many of you reading this book may have also had such experiences. I believe God wanted me to be aware of the spirit realm's existence because people are first spirit beings, then enveloped in flesh. We should all be clear that only with God's guidance and direction should we approach this realm, because spirits of deception, also known as demons, also dwell in the spirit realm.

Demons are disembodied spirits. Intending to possess human vessels to do evil in the earth, they look for people they can influence. I believe this is where most of the crime in our society stems from: demons are using people to commit murder and all types of mayhem — evil personified. These demonic spirits are roaming the earth seeking human beings weak enough to give in to their subliminal suggestions and thoughts to commit the most evil and atrocious deeds.

Many well-meaning, but curious, people have sought information from the dark spirit realm and unknowingly aided demonic spirits that misrepresented themselves and caused havoc in their lives. These people were seduced and tricked into doing evil deeds. Often, by the time they realize this, they have become enslaved to these demonic forces and do not know how to get free. Demons love human beings who crave power, and they will accommodate them. However, the cost is too much for any human being to pay. Many times, the price is their souls, access to their children's future, or even worse. Thankfully, there is help!

Repentance toward God is an absolute must, and it may be necessary to seek deeper help through the ministry of deliverance as well. The devil and his demons are thieves, and their only purpose is found in John 10:10, which reads, "The thief cometh not, but for to steal, and to kill, and to destroy: I am come that they might have life, and that they might have it more abundantly." Jesus is the only remedy. Nothing good comes out of any agreement with the devil or his demons! The Bible states in 1 John 3:8, "He that committeth sin is of the devil; for the devil sinneth from the beginning. For this purpose, the Son of God was manifested, that he might destroy the works of the devil."

While working in the ministry of deliverance, I met a young lady who was extremely troubled. As a child, she had been severely neglected. She had suffered almost every abuse a young girl could experience and had even been sold by her mother to a pimp. She was homeless, with children at a young age, and without a job, when she made a covenant with a demon. She wanted to be the very best strip dancer in the field as a means of notoriety and provision for her family. She had no other skills and had not finished high school. The demons accommodated her. True, she became the best at what she did, second to none. She even attracted movie stars and other very well-known celebrities, and some of them traveled across the country to see her performances. She was worshipped, desired, and idolized by many. Yet, she had no idea of the price she would pay.

Eventually, she became weary of the life she was living. She could not walk down the street without men lusting over her. I witnessed this myself the few times I was around her. In the stores and public places, young men and old men, from every persuasion, were drawn to the spirits within her. Even in church, clergy were also affected. I had never witnessed anything like it before. My first face-to-face encounter with a demon was with one within her. This young lady told me about how she went to a spirit-filled church to get help. The following is her personal testimony:

> While those in the ministry were praying for me, I began crying and I felt movement in my stomach like that of an unborn child. The more they prayed, the more movement I felt in my stomach. Then, I felt an overwhelming urge to throw up! Suddenly, I had no control as my mouth opened so wide that I felt my eyes bulging out of my head! I couldn't close my mouth! It felt like something was moving from the bottom of my stomach up into my throat and then exiting out of my mouth. To me, it was as if a huge snake had come up from the pit of my stomach.

There was a taste in my mouth of dirty fishy water. It was like the smell and taste I had when I was at the reptile house at the zoo as a child. It was a smell and taste I will never forget! When the sensation subsided, I felt some relief as the confusing thoughts I had been having stopped, and I was able to close my mouth. However, I knew that it was not over yet. The pastor also knew it and told me that I needed more ministry and deliverance. He told the people to pick me up for church the next Sunday. (S. Sampson, personal communication, July 5, 2022)

Although she received a small breakthrough, her deliverance was not complete. She had many demons and needed a lot more hands-on ministry. Unfortunately, after the people in the church witnessed her partial deliverance, they became afraid of her and wanted to avoid her at all costs. Because she did not have transportation, she had relied on some of the church members to pick her up for service. They had never encountered anyone in her predicament before and were fearful, so they refused to help her with transportation to the church for further healing and deliverance. She was very discouraged and felt abandoned by the church, reminding her of how her mother had abandoned her as a child. Just when she had a glimpse of hope for deliverance, she was rejected again!

It was obvious to me that the "spirit of rejection" came into her at an early age because of the neglect of her mother. Spirits gain access to children when there is a wound in their emotions. This young lady had suffered so much! She had been deeply wounded by her mother rejecting her — even selling her. This wound attracted the demonic spirit of rejection and many other demons as well. Demons gather in clusters within their victims, each one with its own agenda. Lust, seduction, shame, self-rejection, pride, to name only a few. Of course, the devil took advantage of this last blow from the church, and the young woman went back into the world and her life became even worse. It was a few years later that she came to the church where I was a member.

As mentioned, I began learning about spiritual warfare when I attended Maranatha Ministries, but I was still young in Christ when this young woman came. I allowed my curiosity to get the best of me when I dropped her off at home once and went inside for conversation. I wanted to know more about what was going on with her. Of course, the enemy also knew I was a curious babe in Christ. Somehow during our conversation, I asked a triggering question, and although it seemed innocent, the enemy used it as an opportunity to surface. In deliverance ministry, a *triggering* question is one that would provoke a response from a demon that is present. For the first time, I was looking into the eyes of a heavily oppressed victim. I became very fearful. It was as if I was being hypnotized by this demon that had surfaced, and I felt as if I was falling into a deep, dark hole.

The Holy Spirit within me intervened and told me to "stand up!" She was still in a sitting position. As I stood over her, I began to quote scriptures the Holy Spirit was bringing back to my memory, and the demonic spirits in her backed up from me. For a week or two after that, my mind felt fuzzy. When I asked the Holy Spirit why this was happening, He let me know I had entered into spiritual warfare with the territorial demons that inhabited the young woman. The Holy Spirit gently told me, "You are not ready yet." I knew that meant it was not time for me to minister on that level. Later, the young woman told me of her involvement in the occult. As a result, she would need many sessions of deliverance and inner healing ministry. Years later, I saw her in her right mind and doing well. Glory to God!

Warning! We must be led by the Holy Spirit when we deal with those whom the enemy has under his influence. Also, we should never let our curiosity of the spirit realm get the best of us by consulting with evil practices such as witchcraft, psychics, Ouija boards, games or practices that conjure up evil spirits. Nor should a child of God ever participate in astral projection, séances, or any activity that taps into the dark or demonic realm of the spirit. These are just a few doorways for demons to have access to us. Remember, they want to influence us in order to possess our earthly vessels. It is particularly important for Christians to understand that when we are engaging in sin, we are in the enemy's territory. Involving ourselves in demonic activities gives the enemy the right to attack us because we are in his territory, in which he has authority. However, when we are living a holy life, obedient to God, we do not have to be fearful. Without the hindrance of sin, we are confident in who we represent, and our authority is in the Name and the Blood of our Lord Jesus Christ.

> Behold, I give unto you power to tread on serpents and scorpions, and over all the power of the enemy: and nothing shall by any means hurt you.
>
> — Luke 10:19

> For God hath not given us the spirit of fear; but of power, and of love, and of a sound mind.
>
> — II Timothy 1:7

Velma J. Colston Biggers

Chapter Three

Myths About Spiritual Warfare

It is very important that every believer understand what spiritual warfare is and what it means
to be actively engaged, battling in the spirit. Over
the years, I have heard many definitions of spiritual warfare, and combined with my thoughts and
experiences, I find the following description to be
on point. I believe spiritual warfare is a proactive
response to demonic attack. It is stepping outside
the arena of normal Christian conduct into the
realm of the supernatural, where we depend on
God working through us to dismantle what Satan
has done. Thereby, in the Name of Jesus, we gain
victory. It is declaring war against demonic attacks
purposed to stop us from pursuing Christ.

To successfully engage in spiritual warfare, we
must maintain a close and personal relationship
with the Lord Jesus Christ. We must repent daily

and strive to live according to the Word of God. Apostle Paul said it best in Philippians 3:14, "I press toward the mark for the prize of the high calling of God in Christ Jesus." As children of God, we are disciples of Christ and lifetime subscribers and students of the Word of God.

Because of a lack of understanding or experience, there are many myths about spiritual warfare that believers and unbelievers alike may assume are truth. Several of these myths are addressed below, along with supporting scriptures:

MYTH #1: <u>God has not called everyone to spiritual warfare</u>. Every person; both believers and unbelievers, will encounter spiritual warfare in their lifetime. However, God has commanded and made provision for every believer to be fully equipped to successfully engage in spiritual warfare.

<u>Scripture</u>:

> And these signs shall follow them that believe; In my name shall they cast out devils; they shall speak with new tongues;
>
> — Mark 16:17

> Finally, my brethren, be strong in the Lord, and in the power of his might. Put on the whole armour of God, that ye may be able to stand

against the wiles of the devil. For we wrestle not against flesh and blood, but against principalities, against powers, against the rulers of the darkness of this world, against spiritual wickedness in high places. Wherefore take unto you the whole armour of God, that ye may be able to withstand in the evil day, and having done all, to stand.

— Ephesians 6:10-13

MYTH #2: <u>What you don't know can't hurt you</u>. What you don't know *will* hurt you and can cause destructive forces to be released in your life and in the lives of your loved ones!

> In law, ignorantia juris non excusat (Latin for "ignorance of the law excuses not"), or ignorantia legis neminem excusat ("ignorance of law excuses no one"), is a legal principle holding that a person who is unaware of a law may not escape liability for violating that law merely by being unaware of its content. (Wikipedia. 2021. "Ignorantia juris non excusat. Last modified August 18, 2022)

What you don't know, *can* hurt you. The fact that we may not be aware of generational curses that originated with our ancestors as a result of their disobedience does not resolve or dismiss the resulting curse from inflicting the children. Spiritual warfare gives us the opportunity to address the issue in the spirit realm where it remains open until repentance for the sins of the fathers is made. If we choose not to engage in spiritual warfare, the results can be devastating, crippling, ravishing, and destructive for many, many generations to come. The curse can spiritually afflict until the guilt is resolved through repentance from the responsible party or their representatives. Only then can the curse be lifted. God, because of His great love and compassion, has made a way out for the descendants who love Him but are subjected to the curse as a result of the sins of the fathers.

Scripture:

> Keeping mercy for thousands, forgiving iniquity and transgression and sin, and that will by no means clear the guilty; visiting the iniquity of the fathers upon the children, and upon the children's children, unto the third and to the fourth generation.
>
> — Exodus 34:7

> And the seed of Israel separated themselves from all strangers, and stood and confessed their sins, and the iniquities of their fathers.
>
> — Nehemiah 9:2

MYTH #3: <u>Believers in Christ today are not subject to the laws of the Old Testament</u>. We are not under the law, but we are in the dispensation of grace. Therefore, the Old Testament law does not apply to believers today. However, the Old Testament laws and practices restated in the New Testament (there are many) *are* applicable to the believer today. Jesus fulfilled the laws of the Old Testament, so if we are in Him, we have victory over the law.

The same morals and standards required in the Old Testament still apply today. Failure to uphold these morals and standards required by God will open the door of opportunity for demonic forces to gain access to the child of God. Sin remains the main source of opportunity for demonic attachment, even in the life of the believer. God has not changed His standards.

<u>Scripture</u>:

> Follow peace with all men, and holiness, without which no man shall see the Lord:
>
> — Hebrews 12:14

MYTH #4: <u>A child of God cannot be influenced or affected by a demon</u>. Unrepented sin is the source that will allow demonic presence in the life of the believer as well as the unbeliever. Sin is the root cause of all demonic opportunity. As we will see in the chapter titled, Blessings and Curses, whether the sin is known or unknown in the life of a believer, unrepented sin is an open issue in the spirit realm.

A beautiful sister in the Lord came to me for counseling and was seated across from me. As she spoke, I saw two yellow eyes, surrounded in darkness, peering out at me, from within her. I wondered for a moment if it was my imagination. However, when it blinked, that was confirmation to me that *it* was truly there. I did not feel led by the Holy Spirit to challenge it at that moment. Later, I had a conversation with this sister and determined she was a candidate for counsel with the deliverance ministry. Although she professed belief in the Lord Jesus Christ, she had a demonic presence in her life, and the Holy Spirit within me allowed me to see it.

<u>Scripture:</u>

> And, behold, there was a woman which had a spirit of infirmity eighteen years, and was bowed together, and could in no wise lift herself up.
>
> — Luke 13:11

Earlier in Chapter 13 of the Book of Luke, we find that this woman was a daughter of Abraham, which classifies her as a child of God. Yet, she was bound by a spirit of infirmity. This scripture is confirmation that a child of God can indeed be influenced or bound by demonic spirits. However, because the Holy Spirit dwells within the spirit of the believer, demons cannot influence the believer in their spirit, but they can affect the believer in their flesh and emotions.

MYTH #5: <u>A curse cannot affect believers</u>. In support of this myth, some believers refer to Galatians 3:13; which says, "Christ hath redeemed us from the curse of the law, being made a curse for us: for it is written, Cursed is every one that hangeth on a tree:"

According to biblical law, a child of God cannot be under a curse, but experientially, he or she can. In other words, demons practice squatter's rights. Until a demon is evicted, it can illegally remain. Galatians 3:13 tells us that through the Lord Jesus Christ, the believer can be free from curses. However, we must practice this by legally asserting our authority in Jesus Christ and unseating demonic forces that have trespassed against us. Demons are spiritual squatters, and they take advantage of the fact that authority has not been enforced against them. Many times, spiritual warfare against believers is a direct result of curses operating in our lives without our knowledge.

Scripture:

> Behold, I give unto you power to tread on serpents and scorpions, and over all the power of the enemy: and nothing shall by any means hurt you.
>
> — Luke 10:19

MYTH #6: <u>The Word of God has changed</u>. God's Word has *never* changed and *never* will. If God's Word has changed, that would mean God has changed, for God is one with His Word.

Scripture:

> In the beginning was the Word, and the Word was with God, and the Word was God. The same was in the beginning with God. All things were made by him; and without him was not any thing made that was made.
>
> — John 1:1-3

> For I am the LORD, I change not; therefore ye sons of Jacob are not consumed.
>
> — Malachi 3:6

A WORD OF CAUTION: If you are not a born-again believer in the Lord Jesus Christ, and walking in relationship with Him, or if you question your salvation, you should seek counsel from someone who is knowledgeable and experienced with respect to spiritual warfare before you attempt to engage in spiritual warfare alone.

The following is a biblical example of what happened to someone who did not have a relationship with Christ nor qualifications to engage in spiritual warfare. Acts 19:13-16 reads as follows:

> Then certain of the vagabond Jews, exorcists, took upon them to call over them which had evil spirits the name of the LORD Jesus, saying, We adjure you by Jesus whom Paul preacheth. And there were seven sons of one Sceva, a Jew, and chief of the priests, which did so. And the evil spirit answered and said, 'Jesus I know, and Paul I know; but who are ye?' And the man in whom the evil spirit was leaped on them, and overcame them, and prevailed against them, so that they fled out of that house naked and wounded.

We must use wisdom, which comes from prayer (communing with the Holy Spirit), and study of the Word of God. The Holy Spirit, who is our teacher, will lead and guide us into all truth. As we commit ourselves to God on this level, we will acquire a heavenly knowledge of unseen things.

As believers, we must understand that our warfare comes from three sources: the world, the flesh, and Satan. As a result of the fall of Adam in the Garden of Eden, we live in a cursed and fallen world influenced by Satan and his evil forces. They have one desire, which is to destroy what God cares about most in the earth — that is man. Satan does this by tempting God's creation, man, to sin against his Creator. It is for this reason, the believer is told not to give in to the temptations of the world or flesh, for their only purpose is to gratify the sinful nature of mankind and bring him into bondage for his own destruction. Therefore, it is crucial that we learn to put on the mind of Christ through the Word of God and the leading of the Holy Spirit to avoid all snares leading to demonic bondage.

> And be not conformed to this world: but be ye transformed by the renewing of your mind, that ye may prove what is that good, and acceptable, and perfect, will of God.
>
> — Romans 12:2

> For who hath known the mind of the Lord, that he may instruct him? but we have the mind of Christ.
>
> — 1 Corinthians 2:16

Velma J. Colston Biggers

Chapter Four

My People Perish for Lack of Knowledge

> My people are destroyed for lack
> of knowledge: because thou hast
> rejected knowledge, I will also reject
> thee, that thou shalt be no priest to
> me: seeing thou hast forgotten the
> law of thy God, I will also forget thy
> children.
>
> — Hosea 4:6

*K*nowledge is defined as: "the fact or condition of knowing something with familiarity gained through experience or association." (www.merriam-webster.com.)

I give my testimony in this writing about how I prayed to God that I may know Him. This sincere crying out to God opened the door for me to begin my spiritual journey with the Lord Jesus Christ. God will not turn away from a sincere heart. When we are sincere, He will lead us through His scriptures to His throne. The Word of God becomes our roadmap to the heart of God.

The more we seek God and draw closer to Him, the more familiar we become with His ways. Becoming familiar means we will get to a place in our walk with God where we recognize Him from afar off. There is an example of the disciples walking with Jesus, and even without recognizing Him physically, they could still discern it was Him by characteristics other than those recognizable by sight.

> And they said one to another, Did not our heart burn within us, while he talked with us by the way, and while he opened to us the scriptures?
>
> — Luke 24:32

We need to recognize the Holy Spirit, God's agent in the earth, by what we know about Jesus. How do you recognize the Holy Spirit? What would make you search for Him? We all have an inward desire for *more* and a sense of being incomplete. This exists because God has reserved a secret place in the heart of all mankind just for Himself. Nothing can fill this hole or gap within us except

Him! "The spirit of man is the candle of the LORD, searching all the inward parts of the belly." — Proverbs 20:27

God uses our spirit to enlighten us about Him. Many people believe there is a God, but they do not personally know Him. The only way to know God is through His Word, where He gives us step-by-step instruction and knowledge of how to recognize, know, and engage with Him. He is always engaging with us, yet many do not know it is Him. I can personally attest to the fact that knowing Him is to love Him more than life! It is impossible to know everything about God, because as human beings, we do not have the capacity to take in all that God is. However, I want to receive as much as I can handle!

Years ago, I was at a church for a season and often, when the worship would get high, a certain woman would assume a crippled, bent-over position. Suddenly, she would become unable to talk; her hands would appear shriveled, and she would drag her leg and body as if she was having a seizure. She would get out of her pew and make her way slowly to the front of the church. By this time, all eyes were on her, and she was then the center of attention. Many of the saints of God would encourage her by saying, "That's right, praise Him!" They would work themselves into a frenzy over what should have very easily been discerned as a demonic attempt to steal the worship of God!

Some people really thought this show was the Holy Spirit!

I do not believe this woman was aware the enemy was using her to disrupt the service. She likely thought it was the Holy Spirit moving in her. Nevertheless, this performance interrupted the entire worship service because people were more focused on *her* than on God. I would watch intently, hoping the pastor would stop this demonic show for attention, but he did not.

There was an older gentleman in the congregation, approximately 80 years old, and often our eyes would meet. I could tell he was disgusted with what he saw as well. One day, after a similar scenario with that woman, I saw him shake his head and leave the sanctuary. I never saw him again. We had waited and waited for the pastor to respond because he was the man established over that house. However, he never responded to what was happening.

I know that some people, including me, out of respect for the pastor, did not bind that demon in the Name of Jesus according to Matthew 18:18: "Verily I say unto you, Whatsoever ye shall bind on earth shall be bound in heaven: and whatsoever ye shall loose on earth shall be loosed in heaven."

We felt it was up to the pastor to challenge this demon, stop the foolishness, and restore order to the house! However, if the established man over the house (the pastor), was in agreement with what this woman was doing, binding the devil would have little effect, because the demon using her had the unspoken authority given by the pastor to continue his charade.

Brothers and Sisters, it is crucial that we recognize God for ourselves, lest we be deceived as some of these people were. There were many things that indicated the lack of God's Spirit and order in this house. Along with the example above, this leader stated that God does not talk to his congregation, but rather to him. I bring this up for one reason only, and that is to confirm that people who know their God would not agree with that declaration. Like the true and loving Father He is, God desires to have an intimate one-on-one relationship with each of His children! Our leaders serve God's purpose by ministering His Word, but God's desire is clearly shown throughout His Word — that His people will have personal one-on-one conversations and relationship with Him, and that they know Him for themselves. Our leaders were never meant to replace God in our lives.

> And I will give them an heart to know me, that I am the LORD: and they shall be my people, and I will be their God: for they shall return unto me with their whole heart.
>
> — Jeremiah 24:7

> And they shall teach no more every man his neighbour, and every man his brother, saying, Know the LORD: for they shall all know me, from the least of them unto the greatest of them, saith the LORD: for I will forgive their iniquity, and I will remember their sin no more.
>
> — Jeremiah 31:34

While knowledge of the Word of God is crucial, we must have the understanding and wisdom of the Word to apply it effectively. I discovered there are times we can quote a scripture, without knowing there is a protocol or pre-existing condition that must first be met *before* we can experience the blessing attached to that scripture. We find a clear example in Deuteronomy 28:2, "And all these blessings shall come on thee, and overtake thee, if thou shalt hearken unto the voice of the LORD thy God." It is clear here that God is saying the blessings will come and overtake you *if* you are obedient to His voice.

Here we see that the blessings of God are not always immediate, but sometimes conditional. If we meet the condition of obedience to the Word of God, the blessing is automatically attached to it! We set ourselves up for failure when we do not take the time to thoroughly understand the scriptures. II Timothy 2:15 tells us, "Study to shew thyself approved unto God, a workman that needeth not to be ashamed, rightly dividing the word of truth."

Too often I have witnessed the people of God (including myself), declare the blessings of God upon themselves without having set the ground-work for the blessings to land. We must set the platform for the blessing to land, and that platform is obedience!

> And Samuel said, Hath the LORD as great delight in burnt offerings and sacrifices, as in obeying the voice of the LORD? Behold, to obey is better than sacrifice, and to hearken than the fat of rams.
>
> — 1 Samuel 15:22

Unless we properly apply the Word of God to our lives, the Word becomes like a beautiful song or quote without any real power. It sounds good and strong but is not effective if we do not know how to properly position and connect it to our cir-cumstances. This is why studying the Word, along with communication with the Holy Spirit, is neces-sary. The Holy Spirit will lead us and guide us into all truth. Many people are proud to quote the Bible from beginning to end. However, that means very little if they cannot appropriately apply it to situ-ations in their lives. We need understanding and wisdom to partner with the knowledge of the Word of God.

The Bible tells us in Proverbs 2:6, "For the LORD giveth wisdom: out of his mouth cometh knowledge and understanding."

- Knowledge Is Knowing *WHAT* the Word of God says.
- Understanding Is Knowing *HOW* the Word of God applies to a given situation (operates).
- Wisdom Is Knowing *WHEN* the appropriate time is to apply the Word of God.

Knowledge is crucial for God's children because our knowledge of who Christ is and who we are in Him will determine whether we live in His blessings or live beneath our privileges as children of God. This knowledge affects our ability to claim souls for the Kingdom of God in the earth. As God's legitimate representatives, we must know our God-given authority and understand our assignment to avoid becoming a casualty of *The Invisible War*.

Chapter Five

"The Knowing" — Spiritual Discernment

There is a type of *knowing* that comes from a combination of study, understanding of the Word of God, and being led by the Holy Spirit. This is known as "spiritual discernment." Spiritual discernment is the ability to differentiate truth from error and right from wrong. It is the process of making careful distinctions in our thinking about truth. In other words, the ability to think with discernment is synonymous with the ability to think biblically." I Thessalonians 5:21-22 teaches that it is the responsibility of every Christian to be discerning. "Prove all things; hold fast that which is good. Abstain from all appearance of evil."

The Apostle John issues a similar warning when he says, "Dear friends, do not believe every spirit, but test the spirits to see whether they are from God, because many false prophets have gone out into the world. — 1 John 4:1 (NIV). According to the New Testament, discernment is not optional for the believer, it is required. Knowing God includes being able to discern His ways, behaviors, and voice. The more we walk with God, the more familiar we should become with His ways.

Many years ago, our church leadership team was invited to a sales presentation. Although our pastor did not attend with us, he accepted the invitation on our behalf. We trusted it was something our leader had embraced and, therefore, wanted his leadership team to experience as well. We thought it was awkward and strange that he did not attend with us, nor tell us what it was about beforehand. Nevertheless, we trusted it was for our good. As we entered the building, where the presentation was to be held, we noticed things that caused us to question. There were showcases of crystals of different shapes and sizes, along with paraphernalia that could have been used for the dark arts. Of course, we were shocked, but we tried to be cordial as we felt there had to be a good explanation for it all. There was also a display of items for sale, including various brushes and an odd assortment of other things that appeared to be without suspicion.

When the speaker began his presentation, we expected him, knowing who we were, to connect Jesus to his demonstration. He tried, but he could not do it. I really believe it was the Spirit of God within us, making him very uncomfortable. In the end, we decided to purchase a small brush as a friendly gesture. Truthfully, we should have simply walked away. I thought, *A brush is harmless, right? What happened next was surreal!*"

We stood in line to purchase the brush. There was a large picture behind the counter with bold writing in gold on a black background; it appeared to be Arabic or Middle Eastern. At first glance, it seemed to spell out the name *Jesus*. However, as I looked away from the sign, I felt the urge of the Holy Spirit saying, "Look again!" I responded in a low voice, "It says, *Jesus*." The Holy Spirit repeated, "Look again." This time when I looked, to my surprise, I realized it did not say *J-E-S-U-S* at all, but *E-V-I-L*! I thought I must have been delusional! I asked my husband, who was behind me, to look at the picture and tell me what it said. I did *not* tell him what I saw. His response was, "Jesus." I told him to look again, and he repeated, "Jesus." I told him to look a third time and stunned, he said, "Evil!" At that moment, I recalled the scripture, II Corinthians 13:1 which says, "... in the mouth of two or three witnesses shall every word be established." So, I asked the evangelist, who was ahead of us in line, to read the words. She also said, "Jesus." However, after looking again, she, too, saw the word *Evil*. Without purchasing the brush, we immediately left the line and promptly exited the building!

Our first warning was the crystals and the atmosphere devoid of the Spirit of God. Psychics, witches and others use crystals in their practice of the dark arts. It is possible that someone under demonic influence may have prayed over those items with intent to sell them to do us harm. When we take anything into our home that has been prayed over with demonic intent, it becomes a point of contact for the enemy to gain access to all those within that home. There is no telling what evil our enemy had in store for us! I am so grateful to be able to discern the voice and leading of the Holy Spirit.

Later, we discovered our leader had said that at one time; he was involved in satanic worship. This man was a good preacher, and he was charismatic. He reminded me of a type of Saul, from his stature and demeanor. He *looked* the part of a leader. It does not matter how a person looks or how well a person can perform. We must learn to detect the spirit of a leader, as directed in Matthew 7:15-16. "Beware of false prophets, which come to you in sheep's clothing, but inwardly they are ravening wolves. Ye shall know them by their fruits..."

It is important to know people by their *fruit* to see if they are of God! Just because a person has a title does not mean they are from God! Later, the Lord revealed to me that He did *not* send that man as a pastor. It was a demonic set up; a classic case of a wolf in sheep's clothing.

How devastating that a church leader with questionable motive and behavior sent us there!

My point is that everyone who claims to be from God is not necessarily of God. How can we be effective for the Kingdom of God if we cannot spiritually discern what is of God and what is of Satan? We must have our own personal relationship with the Holy Spirit and fill ourselves with the Word of God so that we will be able to test the spirit to see if it is of God! We left that church, but we continue to pray for the spirit of discernment and for godly leaders in that church and all churches.

Chapter Six

Our Lord Is a Man of War!

Contrary to what some believe, we are not called to be a passive people. According to Exodus 15:3, "The LORD is a man of war: the LORD is his name." Also, Matthew 11:12 reads, "And from the days of John the Baptist until now the kingdom of heaven suffereth violence, and the violent take it by force." From these scriptures, we see our Father as a Man of War and we, like Him, are called to be a conquering people with an aggressive nature pertaining to spiritual warfare and the souls of men. Arming ourselves with the mind of Christ, we are called to evict our enemies by force!

Yet, we do not fight as the world fights. "Stomping on the devil's head" and assailing all types of physical and verbal assaults against the enemy is futile, because our enemy is not physical. He is spiritual. Although we walk in the flesh, we do not fight

Velma J. Colston Biggers   43 against flesh. "(For the weapons of our warfare are not carnal, but mighty through God to the pulling down of strong holds;)" — II Corinthians 10:4

When we properly arm and position ourselves against the enemy with the Word of God, we find God has already made every provision for us to be successful in spiritual warfare.

> Finally, my brethren, be strong in the Lord, and in the power of his might. Put on the whole armour of God, that ye may be able to stand against the wiles of the devil. For we wrestle not against flesh and blood, but against principalities, against powers, against the rulers of the darkness of this world, against spiritual wickedness in high places.
>
> — Ephesians 6:10-12

As believers, our success is dependent upon our knowledge of, and faith in, the Word of God. If we are to be successful, we must be willing to engage in spiritual warfare for ourselves and others against the enemies of God's promises and blessings. God gives us the victory through His Word, but we must first align ourselves with His Word in order to lay hold of that victory. There is a protocol we must adhere to if we want to experience the promises of God. Faith is a key component in battle because without faith, it is impossible to please God! Repentance is another. We must always maintain a repentant heart toward all offenses. An unrepented heart is a powerful attraction for demons.

God is not slack concerning His promises. God has done His part, and fulfilled His promise, through Jesus Christ on the cross, when He said, "It is finished." The rest is up to us. Now, He requires us to take the victory through Christ, along with faith in His Word. We must apply *both* to our circumstances, and put the demonic host in their place, which is under our feet! "Behold, I give unto you power to tread on serpents and scorpions, and over all the power of the enemy: and nothing shall by any means hurt you." — Luke 10:19

There are enemies, squatters in our land, and we are required by God to take up the weapons of our warfare and dispossess all demonic spiritual inhabitants. God holds us responsible for possessing and maintaining the land He has given us. *The land* refers to our mind, body, and soul, along with our families, our homes, and everything He has given us charge over. We must protect and maintain it all, in His Name.

There may be times when we need spiritual reinforcement — which is angelic assistance. God has given us angels to help us, according to scripture: "Are not all angels ministering spirits sent to serve those who will inherit salvation?" — Hebrews 1:14 (NIV)

We must learn to employ the assistance of angels whenever necessary. Many times, I have had to pray and ask God to send His angels against stubborn, demonic oppression. Once, as I awoke from sleep, there were four angels surrounding, holding, comforting me and singing to me. It was amazing! I did not want the experience to end, but as I became more physically conscience and alert, they disappeared.

God is with us! Just because we cannot see or hear Him all the time, does not mean He is not with us. I learned a valuable lesson relating to this when I was a little girl in elementary school. Two bullies chased me home from school. I was terrified as I ran up the stairs of my house, trying to get to safety in the arms of my mother. When I finally made it to my home, my mother came to the door. Those bullies did not care that my mother was at the door; they still pursued me! (The devil is just like that — he is relentless!)

My mother saw what was happening, and she also saw the fear in my eyes. As I ran into the house, to my surprise, she announced that if I did not get back out there and fight them, she would *whoop* me too! *But it was an unfair fight*, I thought. *It was two against one!* They were notorious bullies! However, I saw that my mother meant business! I feared the whooping from my mother more than the beating from these bullies! I had no choice but to turn and run into the bullies with everything I had! My little arms and legs were flinging all over the place, randomly hitting whatever came close. I think I may have closed my eyes at one point. My mom did not stay at the door so I could see her, but I knew she was watching. To my surprise, the bullies ran from me as if they knew I meant business! In fact, one of them became my friend and later turned on the other one.

There have been times, being led by the of the Holy Spirit, when I have sent confusion into the enemy's camp. God will make our enemy our footstool! It is time for His children to stop acting like spiritual wimps, take up the resources God has provided for us, and make the enemy flee! Our Heavenly Father is always watching, and He has our back. He has equipped us to take on our spiritual bullies. We are commissioned to "Put on the whole armour of God, that ye may be able to stand against the wiles of the devil." — Ephesians 6:11

Our Heavenly Father is not worried! He knows we are more than conquerors through Christ Jesus! He knew the end of our story from the very beginning and has planned a way to assure His plan for us will stand — despite what we go through!

Chapter Seven

The Comforter Has Come

> Beloved, now are we the sons of
> God, and it doth not yet appear what
> we shall be: but we know that, when
> he shall appear, we shall be like him;
> for we shall see him as he is.
>
> — 1 John 3:2

This scripture tells us that *now* are we the sons of God. Even though we do not look the part, God's spiritual DNA within us is working to produce children after His own image. When Christ returns, we will see the fulfillment of this scripture, as shown in 1 Corinthians 15:53, "For the perishable must clothe itself with the imperishable, and the mortal with immortality." That means our dying bodies will be transformed into bodies that will never die.

We have God's assurance through His Word; He is working everything out for our good, and when Christ appears, we will be like Him! The child of God can have confidence that regardless of what the beginning looks like, the end will be the result God is expecting. God chose us before He formed the world. His selection of His children is not based upon their goodness, talents or abilities, but the confidence that God has in His own Word — His expected end! "For I know the thoughts that I think toward you, saith the LORD, thoughts of peace, and not of evil, to give you an expected end." — Jeremiah 29:11

Since God is Light, then we, His children, are the children of Light! Many claim to be children of God, but in reality, while we are all part of God's creation, we are not all necessarily sons of God. The litmus test, without a doubt, is the Holy Spirit living within us. Only those who have God's Spirit, the Holy Spirit, are the sons of God. Romans 8:14 tells us, "For as many as are led by the Spirit of God, they are the sons of God."

Being a child of God requires more than confessing Jesus Christ as our Lord and Savior. We must invite the Holy Spirit to dwell within us. In order to be on one accord with God, we need the Holy Spirit, the divine connection, to help us understand spiritual things. "Now we have received, not the spirit of the world, but the spirit which is of God; that we might know the things that are freely given to us by God." — 1 Corinthians 2:12

Improper teaching about being filled with the Holy Spirit can be a source of confusion for young believers and can lead to spiritual attack. The enemy has led people to believe the following:

- You do not have to be filled with the Holy Spirit.
- Believing is all that matters.
- You already have the Holy Spirit.
- It does not take all that!

Our enemy uses all these excuses and more to bring confusion, fear, and discord to the believer. My personal testimony is that I want everything God has for me! In Acts 2:38, the Bible tells us that we will receive the gift of the Holy Spirit. The Holy Spirit is a promise of God. II Corinthians 1:20 assures us that God will honor all His promises, for all His promises in Christ Jesus are *yes* and *amen*.

While there is some disagreement about speaking in tongues, again, I say, "I want everything God has for me!" In my experience, being filled with the Holy Spirit, with speaking in tongues, has been and continues to be one of the greatest weapons in spiritual warfare. The enemy tried his best to discourage me from experiencing the power of praying in tongues. I asked God to fill me with His Spirit, according to Act 2:38, with the evidence of speaking in tongues, and He did! "And these signs shall follow them that believe; In my name shall they

cast out devils; they shall speak with new tongues;"
— Mark 16:17

When I communicate with God in my heavenly language, immediately I am in His presence. I would never trade this level of intimacy with God for anything in this world! I understand why the devil fights the people of God to discourage them from speaking in their heavenly language. Today, I continue to spend intimate time with the Lord, praying with understanding, as well as praying in tongues.

The bottom line is that we need the Holy Spirit to dwell within us. The Word of God makes it clear that if we don't have the Holy Spirit within us, regardless of what we say, we are not His.

> But ye are not in the flesh, but in the Spirit, if so be that the Spirit of God dwell in you. Now if any man have not the Spirit of Christ, he is none of his.
>
> — Romans 8:9

One day, on my way home from work, the Holy Spirit told me to make a detour to my mother's home. He did not say why, I just obediently followed His command. It was a beautiful summer day, and as I arrived in front of my mom's home, I heard a voice, from a short distance, call my name. It was my sister, Elaine, walking down the street toward me with a young man. She told him, "That is who you need to talk to. Maybe she can help you!" I had no idea what the Lord was getting me into. She introduced the young man, and he almost immediately began to defend his position about why it was not necessary to speak in tongues. As I listened to him, I could tell he was getting angry about this topic. I continued listening, discerning what God was doing. Then the Holy Spirit let me know this young man was angry at God because he had not been able to speak in tongues. So, he wanted to challenge me on the Word of God concerning speaking in tongues.

Shortly into our conversation, the Holy Spirit told me repentance was necessary for him. He did not resist. He repented and the Holy Spirit gave me a few scriptures to share with him. The next thing I knew, this young man began praising God right there in the middle of the sidewalk, in broad daylight! Almost immediately, his language changed, and he spoke beautifully and powerfully in his heavenly language! It was one of the most beautiful things I had ever witnessed! I still get goose bumps reflecting on that day. God showed up in broad daylight, on the sidewalk, on a residential street. People were bustling about, but it was as if they did not see us. This young man spoke powerfully in several dialects of tongues! To this day, I have heard nothing more beautiful than the Holy Spirit speaking through this young man. In amazement, I witnessed a river of tears flowing down his face.

With his hands lifted toward heaven, he continued in that posture for over twenty minutes. All I could do was marvel and say, "Look what God has done!" I believe the scriptures God had brought to my mind to share with him caused this young man to release his faith in God. That was the reason for his breakthrough — it was faith! I understood why the enemy fought him so fiercely about speaking in tongues. He wanted to rob him of this powerful experience! Slowly, the young man came around, conscious enough to continue on his way, so full and so very grateful. Still praising God and speaking in his new heavenly language, he nodded his head toward me (I received it as his way of saying "thank you"). He turned and walked back in the direction he had come from. I never saw him again, and neither did my sister. That day, this son of God, had a divine appointment with his Heavenly Father. I was blessed to serve as a type of midwife and witness the power of what faith in the Word of God will do!

> "And these signs shall follow them that believe; In my name shall they cast out devils; they shall speak with new tongues;"
>
> — Mark 16:17

Velma J. Colston Biggers

"But as many as received him, to them gave he power to become the sons of God, even to them that believe on his name."

— John 1:12

God has provided everything needed for the believer to make it into the Kingdom of Heaven. Even giving His Spirit, who is the Holy Spirit, the Comforter, the guide and source of power to become His children.

Chapter Eight

The Demonic Host: Satan and Demons

I have heard it said, "Don't talk about the devil, also known as Satan, because you will give him too much power!" I disagree, because at some time or another he (or his demons) must become a part of our conversation. If we are to successfully engage with a spiritual and intellectual being, who has been around for thousands of years before mankind, it is to our advantage to know something about him. We gain this knowledge through the scriptures and the leading of the Holy Spirit. Our enemy, Satan, uses deception as his main weapon of offense and defense. One of the most powerful myths he has propagated is that he does not exist. All the while, the Bible confirms that he does, and he is alive and well today.

Because he is so deceptive, it is all the more important that we know what he is able to do, his limitations, and the various ways in which he works. We know for a fact that Satan takes advantage of those who are spiritually immature. Our enemy thrives on our ignorance; he is ruthless and calculating. He has no respect for man, woman, or child. Jesus tells us of Satan's main objective in John 10:10: "The thief cometh not, but for to steal, and to kill, and to destroy: I am come that they might have life, and that they might have it more abundantly."

Satan and demons thrive on what we do not know. The demonic host is not holding back, waiting for us to discern his activity, but rather violently opposes us every day! Who is Satan? The Bible tells us in John 8:44, which reads,

> ...He was a murderer from the beginning, and abode not in the truth, because there is no truth in him. When he speaketh a lie, he speaketh of his own: for he is a liar, and the father of it.

Satan, or the devil "(from Greek diabolos, 'slanderer' or 'accuser'), the spirit or power of evil. Though sometimes used for minor demonic spirits, the word devil generally refers to the prince of evil spirits and as such takes various forms in the religions of the world." (www.britannica.com). Demons are disembodied evil spirits, seeking a body through whom they can carry out their evil deeds in the earth. Unlike God, they are not omnipresent (able to be in all places at all times). Unlike God, they cannot read the minds of human beings, as confirmed by our Lord in Matthew 9:4, which reads, "And Jesus knowing their thoughts said, Wherefore think ye evil in your hearts?"

Satan is a being created by God. Whereas God *always* existed. God has no beginning or ending. In the book of Genesis, we see that God, the Creator, set specific laws in place concerning how the earth was supposed to function and he set man as earth's caretaker along with Himself. In Genesis, we see how man listened to Satan, who, disguised as a serpent, convinced mankind to disobey God. As a result, the world fell and continues to spiral away from God's original plan. However, regardless of what it may look like, Satan is a defeated foe. God's Word still trumps everything, regardless of how things may appear.

> So shall my word be that goeth forth out of my mouth: it shall not return unto me void, but it shall accomplish that which I please, and it shall prosper in the thing whereto I sent it.
> — Isaiah 55:11

Because Satan cannot stop God's plans, he and his demonic hosts' main focus is to corrupt and destroy God's creation — man, who is made in the image of God. They do this best if they have access to human bodies. They are very desperate, so if they cannot inhabit a human body, they will temporarily settle for being housed in an animal's body. Their main objective is to have a body in which they can function in the natural world, making them somewhat *legal* to cause dysfunction and mayhem wherever they can. A great example of their desperation for bodies is found in Matthew 8:28-32:

> And when he was come to the other side into the country of the Gergesenes, there met him two possessed with devils, coming out of the tombs, exceeding fierce, so that no man might pass by that way. And, behold, they cried out, saying, What have we to do with thee, Jesus, thou Son of God? art thou come hither to torment us before the time? And there was a good way off from them an herd of many swine feeding. So the devils besought him, saying, If thou cast us out, suffer us to go away into the herd of swine. And he said unto them, Go. And when they were come out, they went into the herd of swine: and, behold, the whole herd of swine ran violently down a steep place into the sea, and perished in the waters.

Velma J. Colston Biggers

Their purpose is clear — destruction! When the demons entered into the swine, the swine were driven into madness and to their own destruction. That is what Satan and demons do! Yet, for the believer, 1 John 4:4 tells us, "Ye are from God, little children, and have overcome them: because greater is he that is in you, than he that is in the world." We have no reason to be fearful of Satan or demons as God has given us power and authority over all our enemies so that nothing shall by any means hurt us.

By reading Revelation 20:10, we learn that Satan is a defeated enemy, one who ultimately will be thrown into the lake of fire. However, until that time, he is still very active in this world.

Chapter Nine

The Spirit of Divination

There shall not be found among
you any one that maketh his son
or his daughter to pass through the
fire, or that useth divination, or an
observer of times, or an enchanter,
or a witch. Or a charmer, or a con-
sulter with familiar spirits, or a wiz-
ard, or a necromancer. For all that
do these things are an abomination
unto the LORD: AND BECAUSE OF
THESE ABOMINATIONS THE LORD
THY GOD DOTH DRIVE THEM OUT
FROM BEFORE THEE.

— Deuteronomy 18:10-12

I chose to discuss this particular spirit because of my personal experience with it. I witnessed the destruction and devastation that can come from engaging with this spirit. More importantly, the Lord allowed me to witness the victory of overcoming it as well. I want the world to know, DO NOT SEEK ANY INFORMATION FROM PEOPLE WHO ARE CONNECTED WITH THIS SPIRIT! No matter how well they are disguised or how innocent they appear, do not seek counsel from them!

Too often people are not patient enough to wait on God to give them answers to life's problems. Instead, they seek answers from alternative sources, having no idea of the impact this will have on their lives and the lives of their families. Those alternative sources include psychics, witches, warlocks, tarot card readers, and all who practice any form of divination. Also included are items used for divination, such as numerology, crystals, essential oils, signs and signals, stream-of-consciousness writing, and others. *Divination* is defined as "the art or practice that seeks to foresee or foretell future events or discover hidden knowledge usually by the interpretation of omens or by the aid of supernatural powers." (www.merriam-webster.com)

Divination is a dangerous practice that will have a negative impact on the lives of those who participate in it. We need to consult the Holy Spirit, who is the Spirit of Truth, to teach us who we are through the Word of God and to direct our steps in this world. The Word of God says, in John 16:13, *He* will show you things to come.

> Howbeit when he, the Spirit of truth, is come, he will guide you into all truth: for he shall not speak of himself; but whatsoever he shall hear, that shall he speak: and he will shew you things to come.

There are many people who are curious and seek understanding about their current and future state in this life, so much so, that they seek information from those who practice divination instead of seeking God.

Divination is:

> (from Latin *divinare*, 'to foresee, to foretell, to predict, to prophesy') is the attempt to gain insight into a question or situation by way of an occultic, standardized process or ritual. Used in various forms throughout history, diviners ascertain their interpretations of how a querent should proceed by reading signs, events, or omens, or through alleged contact with a supernatural

agency. (Wikipedia. 2022. "Divination." Last modified August 6, 2022)

The above article also states, "Divination (from
Latin *divinare* 'to foresee, to be inspired by a god',
related to *divinus*, divine) is the attempt to gain
insight into a question or situation by way of an
occultic, standardized process or ritual." Please
note that although the article states "inspired by a
god," this does *not* refer to God.

The Bible makes it clear that consulting these
sources is an abomination unto the Lord. We must
learn to submit ourselves with faith and patience
to the Holy Spirit, who knows all things. He can
speak directly to us (in our spirit), or He can send
a messenger from among us. "The LORD thy God
will raise up unto thee a Prophet from the midst
of thee, of thy brethren, like unto me; unto him ye
shall hearken." — Deuteronomy 18:15

When the Holy Spirit chooses to communicate with us concerning our situation, the mes-
sage will come directly from God's heart. I will
be transparent in sharing my personal testimony
about my encounter with a palm reader. My hope
is that someone will take heed and save themselves from a terrible experience, such as I had,
although at the time of my visit, I did not know of
the consequences.

My Personal Visit to a Palm Reader

Years ago, before I gave my life to the Lord Jesus Christ and received apostolic teaching, I agreed with a friend of mine to visit a palm reader. I had absolutely no idea what it was all about and did it simply to prevent her from going alone. We arrived at this older woman's home, who promised, for a fee, to give people information about their present and future. There were crucifixes on the walls and Bibles placed around the room, which impressed me. I thought perhaps she was Catholic, and this could not be all bad. There was also a picture of Mary, the mother of Jesus, on the wall. A little child, around three years old, was running around the room. I was told she had the gift of reading palms and prophesy and was already using her gifts to foretell the future. There were other people moving about outside of the room, while the woman read different people's palms inside. I did not see any devils running around, no horns on the palm reader's head, and I heard no satanic music playing. The room was not dark, gloomy, or spooky. It all seemed so innocent. She proceeded to read my palm and tell me things she felt she knew about me. Some of it was on point. However, when she said I would have another child, I laughed to myself, because that was not in our plans. In fact, we were practicing birth control to prevent that. I was definitely convinced she did not know what she was talking about, and I disregarded what she said.

Several years later, I was surprised to discover I was pregnant! The first thought that came to my mind and I spoke aloud was, "The reader said I would have another baby!" I had no idea what I had just done! I had agreed with an enemy of God! Unknowingly, I immediately gave permission for a curse to come upon me and my unborn child. I had just started receiving Apostolic teaching but was still considered a *babe.* I had so much more to learn about spiritual things. I didn't know then that I had given the enemy access to my unborn child! This may seem farfetched to some, but I am speaking truth. The Word of God is very clear about divination. It is written in Deuteronomy 18:10, "There shall not be found among you any one that maketh his son or his daughter to pass through the fire, or that useth divination, or an observer of times, or an enchanter, or a witch."

After my child was born, we noticed that when he was in church and the Word of God was being read or the sermon was being preached, he would cry for no reason. The pastor's wife discerned that my child was being tormented by a demonic spirit. One evening, my pastors came over to our home for dinner, along with another guest. Our son, who was then three years old, was upstairs playing in his room. As he came down the steps, he did something I had never seen him do before. He started screaming and went into a fit, shouting, "I told you she could not come here!" (He was referring to the female guest.)

When my husband and the pastor tried to restrain him from hurting himself, we witnessed him exhibit supernatural strength by resisting and throwing grown men, the pastor and my husband away from him! I say supernatural because there was no way a three-year-old should have been able to hurl these grown men around! We did not know it at the time, but the evil spirits attached to him knew they were about to be evicted. Thank God my pastors had the gift of discernment and were also gifted in the ministry of deliverance. They knew how to pray and release knowledge from the Holy Spirit so my son would be set free. It was terrifying! If I had not seen this for myself, it would be hard to believe!

We prayed and my pastor's wife said; "Sister Biggers, this has something to do with you." I calmed myself and opened my heart and ears to hear from the Holy Spirit. In a very small still voice, I heard Him say, "You went to the reader." Immediately, I said, "I know what it is. I went to see a reader!" My pastor's wife said, "That's it! Repent in the Name of Jesus!" As I looked into the eyes of my child, I could sense there was something else present, waiting to see if I had the key to dismiss it. I said, "I am so sorry, Jesus, that I went to see that palm reader and I repent in Jesus' Name!"

I was so grieved because I knew I had caused torment to my child, and I had offended God! After I repented, my pastors instructed me to tell the demon to go! I said with authority, "Go now in the

Name of Jesus!" The demon left immediately! My son's whole demeanor changed as he said, "Mommy, she can stay now." I had my three-year-old son back to normal again, praise God! Later, I remembered there were several incidents that occurred while I was pregnant with my son that could have led to a miscarriage. It all made sense now!

Repentance removed the legal right I had given the demon by visiting the palm reader. I realize now that I had counseled with a familiar spirit — a demon. When I talk about this incident, I still feel anger at how the enemy took advantage of my lack of knowledge, and I still feel very badly about my decision to seek counsel from a demonic source. I sometimes tremble as I consider what could have happened to my child if God had not mercifully forgiven me and given us divine knowledge of how to evict this demon. I learned the hard way. I did not know, but now, those reading this testimony will be without excuse.

I believe it was just a coincidence that the palm reader said I would have another child; I was still very young. The problem began when I agreed with what she said. I believe at the point of my agreement with the reader, I unknow-ingly entered into a demonic covenant and the enemy attacked my unborn child who was grow-ing inside my womb as payment for my disobe-dience to God. Please be careful what you agree with and what you *amen*. By agreeing with the palm reader, I agreed with someone who got their information from a demonic source, a familiar spirit to be exact, and a curse entered into my life and the life of my unborn child. This consultation broke God's commandment. Who knows what destruction lay ahead for my family if God had not intervened on our behalf? There is a steep price to pay when we consult psychics and readers. Regardless of how they try to make what they do appear innocent, it is not! Some of them may not be aware of the havoc they can send into the lives of those they service.

You may ask, "How did she know some things about you that were true?" That is because psychics, palm readers, soothsayers, and the like, practice divination. That is, they get their information from familiar spirits who have been around for many generations. Unlike true prophets who get their information from the Holy Spirit, psychics, soothsayers, and fortune tellers get their information from the dark or demonic realm.

The Bible calls them familiar because they are familiar with our families. They have followed our families for many generations, and they know our family history. For this reason, they can tell you information you may not know about your great-great-grandparents and their deeds. The intent is always to gain your confidence and trust so that you will follow them and not the voice of God. This is what God says about those who consult familiar spirits:

> And the soul that turneth after such as have familiar spirits, and after wizards, to go a whoring after them, I will even set my face against that soul, and will cut him off from among his people.
>
> — Leviticus 20:6

Those who practice divination as well as those who consult the practitioner will pay a very heavy penalty according to the scripture above. Although some of the names or titles of those who practice divination have changed today, their purpose is still the same and that is to persuade you to trust in them instead of God. How many people will call the psychic hotline instead of Jesus? I see many people deceived by this spirit, unaware of the consequences that "friendly visit" will cause them and their families. If God had not allowed me to be with such knowledgeable pastors, I cannot imagine what my visit would have opened up in our lives. If this demon had not been cast out, no doubt it would have presented itself to at least the third and fourth generations of my family.

The devil and demons take joy in what we do not know. When you know the darkness connected with psychics, soothsayers, witches, and others, you will avoid them at all costs. God allowed it to be personal for me, so I would be passionate about this topic and be a witness to you. After I witnessed the power of God move in my situation with my son, I embraced the authority God has given the believer.

I was at a flea market one day, when I noticed people standing in line to see the psychics. They were waiting for the psychics, also known as *readers,* to set up camp to give psychic readings. The Lord told me to send the spirit of confusion into the midst of the readers, so the psychics could not get information from their demonic source. Very quietly, I said, "In the Name of Jesus, Lord, send the spirit of confusion into the psychics' camp. Do not allow them to receive information from the demonic realm." The Lord allowed me to see how effective my prayer request was. After those who were waiting had their visit with the readers, they complained that they did not receive anything of value or truth from them. That was the intent of my prayer, that they would not give the people anything to cause them to have confidence in psychics or those who practice divination.

God has allowed some witnesses into our lives so we will be without excuse for disobedience. Do not discard their warnings, as the consequences can be severe. If you have ever consulted with psychics, readers or similar people who claim the power to *know* or *foretell,* repent now in the Name of Jesus! It does not matter how long ago it was... repent! Just because you have not witnessed the consequences of that visit, it is not too late for the fruit of that visit to appear in your life or the lives of your loved ones. Remember, we are citizens of the

Kingdom of Heaven. Our allegiance is to God only.
Seek the Holy Spirit and He will lead you and guide
you into all truth.

Chapter Ten

Blessings and Curses

I call heaven and earth to record this day against you, that I have set before you life and death, blessing and cursing: therefore choose life, that both thou and thy seed may live:

— Deuteronomy 30:19

But it shall come to pass, if thou wilt not hearken unto the voice of the LORD thy God, to observe to do all his commandments and his statutes which I command thee this day; that all these curses shall come upon thee, and overtake thee:

— Deuteronomy 28:15

Many people have the wrong impression of what it means to be blessed by God. It is not how much property you own. It is not even the amount of money you have in the bank that determines whether you are blessed. To be blessed means to be recognized and accepted by God. God's blessing, according to scripture, is total well-being. It is salvation, healing, deliverance, strength, provision, abundance, victory over our enemies, wisdom, revelation, knowledge, and understanding. It is also God's desire that His blessings in our life be limitless!

On the opposite end of the spectrum are curses. In my research, I have come to understand a curse to be the result of an evil pronouncement upon a person. Curses involve speaking words intended to produce negative results. This would even include speaking evil against *ourselves*. We must be careful not to speak every word that comes to our minds, regardless of our emotions at the time. We must agree with what God has said about us. Failure to do so could change the DNA of our thought process, prohibiting us from becoming what God intended for us to be. When God spoke a thing, it manifested. We have that same potential; to speak a thing into existence. Words have real power. God spoke the world into existence by the power of His Words. We reflect His image, in part, because of the power we have with words. "Through faith we understand that the worlds were framed by the word of God, so that things which are seen were not made of things which do appear." — Hebrews 11:3

A generational curse is believed to be passed down from one generation to another. Iniquity, which is rebellion against God, stands at the root of curses and it provides the means for curses to come upon the descendants. If your family line is marred by divorce, incest, poverty, anger, or other ungodly patterns, your family may be functioning under a generational curse. The Bible says that these curses are tied to choices.

> The LORD is longsuffering, and of great mercy, forgiving iniquity and transgression, and by no means clearing the guilty, visiting the iniquity of the fathers upon the children unto the third and fourth generation.
>
> — Numbers 14:18

Demons are attracted to sin in a person's life or unrepented ancestral sin. Two things are necessary for a demon to occupy a person. First, they must locate a point of entry. This will be through a person's invitation or through an emotional or spiritual weakness in the person. Just like the example of the young lady, in the earlier chapter titled, "The Spirit Realm," who consciously entered into a covenant with a demon in exchange for greatness, the price to pay for such an agreement is unimaginable. It is a debt that cannot be satisfied with all the money in the world because the price to pay could be your very soul or your children's quality of life!

Second, there must be a legal right for the demon to stay there. Demons gain a legal right when there is no objection to their presence. Just like a squatter, they will stay until they are legally evicted. Demons cannot just randomly attach to a person. There must be an invitation from the person that will allow the demon access. That invitation may be conscience or unconscious. The conscience invitation would include involvement and practice with groups that worship gods or powers other than the true God. This would include, but not be limited to; those involved in the occult, those who participate in seeking spirit guides, channeling, New Age Movement, Freemasonry, Christian Science, Jehovah Witnesses, Satanists, just to name a few. All require a person to make a conscience decision to listen to, agree with and participate in the core values adopted by these groups. By doing so, you are making a conscience decision to practice and entertain what comes along with it. Unknowingly, this can include demonic attachments.

Practices such as the following also fall within the conscience invitation: attending séances, going to fortune tellers, being involved in levitation, playing with occult-oriented games, and using tarot cards. All involve occult practices and open the door to demonic activity, putting a person in danger of demonic oppression, depression, and the last state of possession. Many people do not know that being involved with the practices of these groups endanger not only themselves, but their families as well.

The unconscious invitation usually occurs when a person is wounded physically or emotionally, and they carry a negative attitude from the experience and cannot move past it. For example, they become angry. Anger leads to unforgiveness, and if a person clings to it, it can progress to resentment or bitterness. Envy, worry, fear, alcohol abuse, self-hate, drugs, lustful thoughts, unconfessed sin, addictive behavior, pornography, sexual sins, or unforgiveness would also classify as unconscious invitations. These actions produce spiritual trash, which weakens our spiritual defense and attracts demons, giving them opportunity to enter.

Our families have the greatest influence on our development, including patterns of sin that are passed down through generations. We inherit many traits from our parents that aren't always positive. When we acquire sinful habits or beliefs from our families, that negatively affects our lives or those around us, this is known as a generational curse. It is the shadow side of behavior passed down through the generations. However, through Jesus Christ, it *is* possible to break this cycle of pain and suffering.

Remember a demon's greatest advantage over man is deception. Demons intentionally cause their works to appear attractive to gain our attention and confidence. Freemasonry is a good example. This is an organization whose members may outwardly claim to be Christian, but within its practices, core tenets of Christianity do not appear to be revered, upheld, or followed.

I have spoken to people who are involved in this group, and they are led to believe it is biblical or based on Christian values. However, a close look at what they practice and ascribe to conflicts with Christian values. For example, Freemasons believe that members can serve other gods, meaning the god of their choice. Christianity specifically ascribes to the only true God — Jesus Christ. Consider the following statements about Freemasonry from well-known, longstanding Christian churches and organizations:

> It is because tenets and practices of Freemasonry conflict with the biblical Gospel of Jesus Christ that our church from its very beginning has held that membership in this organization conflicts with a faithful confession of this Gospel.
>
> — Lutheran Church Missouri Synod

> Confidence in these secret orders and their teachings has always tended toward the embracing of a

false hope of salvation through good
works and improved moral service
(Eph. 2:8-9).

— Assemblies of God

Ex-Masons for Jesus is an organization of
Christian men and women who were once mem-
bers of a Masonic Lodge or one of the affiliated
Masonic organizations, including Eastern Star.
Following are excerpts from a testimony found on
their website:

We have left Masonry because of our
commitment to Jesus Christ and a
realization that Masonry is not con-
sistent with a sincere expression of
the Christian faith. We have found
that participation in Freemasonry
interferes with a close relationship
with Jesus Christ." According to
Ex-Masons for Jesus, while Freemason require its members to believe
in the existence of a Supreme Being
and that there is only One God,
Freemasonry refers to its god as the
Great Architect of the Universe.
Their belief system teaches that all
men even though they are of different religions, worship one God simply using different names. Therefore,

Masons may be Hindus, Moslems, or men who follow Jesus. Our bible specifically states "I am the LORD, and there is no other, apart from me there is no God. Isaiah 45:5. (D. Washum, www.emfj.org)

Duane Washum is a former Worshipful Master and he gives his testimony that he left the Free Masons because their practices were not Christian based. He gives his testimony on several platforms including Facebook. He speaks of how he came to the truth of Freemasonry and denounced it because it does not line up with Christianity. He and many others who have denounced Free Masonry now seek to expose the non-Christian teachings of Freemasonry. They even go so far as to make themselves available to witness and testify of our firsthand knowledge. (www.emfj.org)

Years ago, I worked in the insurance industry, and I had to evaluate damages to people's homes to compensate them after they suffered a loss. One day, while in the field, I entered a customer's home. I could feel an evil presence inside. I shrugged it off as the possibility of being tired, as it was the end of the day. As I moved around the home taking measurements, I heard the Holy Spirit tell me to "bind up a spirit of murder." My back was to the customer at that moment. I did not question the Holy Spirit, because I know His voice. In a whisper, I said "In the Name of Jesus, I bind you, Spirit of Murder!" I knew I did not have to speak loudly; demons hear well.

Immediately after I spoke, I casually turned toward this man, to see him approaching me from behind. He was sweating profusely as I faced him, and I could see that something had come over him. It was a dramatic change. He looked confused and tried to smoke a cigarette to calm himself. A demonic spirit was brought to a halt, but the man did not understand what was happening. The Lord drew my attention to items hanging on the wall, which explained everything. This man was a high-ranking Freemason. I believe he was also possessed. If people really knew what they were pledging themselves to and who they were making covenants with, they would have nothing to do with these groups. When I got to my car, I rejoiced because truly greater is He who is in me than he that is in the world!

During a church service, I had another experience with a man at the altar. The Lord told me to call this man up for prayer. When he came up to me, I felt a spiritual block like I had never experienced before. It was like a brick wall. I asked the Lord, "Why did you have me call him to prayer?"

Velma J. Colston Biggers

The Lord told me to look around the man's neck. I saw the Freemason symbol and the Lord told me this is what happens to them. Their heart becomes as hard as a brick wall toward the things of God. I prayed that God would break through this man's stony heart and give him a heart of flesh. Many Freemasons are proud to be high ranking and generational. The sad thing is that many believe they are saved. People need to be aware of the dangers associated with secret societies.

Every person has 30 people involved in their destiny before they arrive on the earth: Two parents, four grandparents, eight great-grandparents, and sixteen great-great-grandparents. These are the people who have made decisions in their lifetimes that can and do affect their families. Who knows what shadows and skeletons lurk in their closets, and have been passed down to their descendants? While we must shut the door to personal sin, it is crucial that we shut the door to ancestral sins as well.

Every person whose ancestors participated in sinful behavior that they did not repent for, may be affected by their failure to do so. However, the solution is found in Nehemiah 9:2 "And the seed of Israel separated themselves from all strangers, and stood and confessed their sins, and the sins of their fathers." By the people confessing the sins of the fathers, *they* also repented for those sins. As a result, we find God's mercy upon the descendants of the guilty in Exodus 34:7.

> Keeping mercy for thousands, for-
> giving iniquity and transgression
> and sin, and that will by no means
> clear the guilty; visiting the iniquity
> of the fathers upon the children,
> and upon the children's children,
> unto the third and to the fourth
> generation.

We must not forget, we have the Comforter on board, the Holy Spirit who will lead and guide us into all truth. God does not want to withhold any of His blessings from His children. Therefore, if we ask the Holy Spirit what sins our ancestors have committed that opened doors and allowed curses into our life, He will answer us. I stand today as a witness!

One night, as I was settling down in bed, the Holy Spirit brought something back to my mind. When I was a little girl around six or seven years of age, I had terrible nose bleeds. My loving grand-mother would take me out in the yard, find a spot in the dirt, and dig a cross in the ground with a tree branch. She instructed me to bend over to allow the blood from my nose to collect in the cross drawn in the dirt, until my nose stopped bleeding. I thought this practice was to stop the nose bleeds; therein lies the danger. God does not want us to seek help from any source other than Him. Just like putting salt in the corners of the house will not keep demons out, neither will a cross drawn in the dirt stop nose bleeds. They are traditions of men. God does not want us to practice these traditions, because they cause people to stray away from God and put their confidence in false hope, the traditions of men.

I had no idea my dear relative, who loved God, had offended Him. I am sure she didn't know either, or else she wouldn't have done it. At the very least, she would have repented from it. The Holy Spirit so lovingly let me know this was still a standing issue in the spirit realm that had to be resolved. I repented for the sins of my fathers; in this case, my grandmother.

> For laying aside the commandment
> of God, ye hold the tradition of men,
> as the washing of pots and cups: and
> many other such like things ye do.
>
> — Mark 7:8

Chapter Eleven

Salvation versus Sanctification

I once thought that through repentance for personal sin (baptism), I had arrived at the land of milk and honey in Christ Jesus. Baptism, identifies me with Jesus' death, burial and resurrection, and the infilling of the Holy Spirit, God within me. Yet, I do not understand why I still suffer from some of the same issues I had before I received the Lord Jesus Christ! I still struggle with evil thoughts, temptations, rejection, shame, mental torment and other things I thought I would never have to experience again! What am I missing? Am I really saved?"

— Anonymous

We are saved when we embrace Jesus's death, burial and resurrection. We have become heirs to salvation. Jesus establishes our victory through Him in Revelation 1:18, "I am he that liveth, and was dead; and, behold, I am alive for evermore, Amen; and have the keys of hell and of death." Although we are saved from hell and death, our current struggle is with our flesh. The demonic realm does all it can to dominate, weaken, distract, and discourage human beings, in an effort to control and manipulate the children of God and prevent us from walking in our purpose in the earth.

When we are born again, our spirit man becomes alive, but our flesh is exactly the same as it was before; it is still sinful and full of lusts. This is because when we received the Lord as our Savior, we were born again in our human spirit with the divine Spirit of God, but our flesh, our bodies, remain the same. For as long as we live in this physical life, the sinful nature of our flesh; the "old man," remains the same. There will always be temptation and struggle, no matter how long we're saved or how much we've grown in the Lord. "That which is born of the flesh is flesh; and that which is born of the Spirit is spirit." — John 3:6

Apostle Paul said in Romans 7:25, "I thank God through Jesus Christ our Lord. So then with the mind I myself serve the law of God; but with the flesh the law of sin." Only when the Lord Jesus returns will we be rid of the flesh by God's resurrecting and transfiguring our fallen bodies. Philippians 3:20-21 tells us:

> For our conversation is in heaven; from whence also we look for the Saviour, the Lord Jesus Christ: Who shall change our vile body, that it may be fashioned like unto his glorious body, according to the working whereby he is able even to subdue all things unto himself.

God's full salvation plan, which He promised in His Word, includes our flesh. For now, our flesh remains sinful. The flesh, which is a term for body and soul, needs to be sanctified. Sanctification is a life-long process. To be fully sanctified is to be like Jesus. His Spirit in us does the work of sanctification as we submit to Him daily. Believers who do not understand the sanctification process remain babes in their spirits. To grow in the spirit, one needs to be filled with the Holy Spirit and walk according to His instructions. The Holy Spirit lives within us and leads and guides us. He is our Helper, Comforter, and Teacher. He is always communicating His thoughts and feelings to us. All we need to do is listen and obey Him. Romans 12:2 tells us, "And be not conformed to this world: but be ye transformed by the renewing of your mind, that ye may prove what is that good, and acceptable, and perfect, will of God."

When we acknowledge Jesus as Lord, we invite the Holy Spirit to take over. This is a daily surrender to His will. The devil, our flesh, and the world conspire to distract us from our submission to the Lord. Although God is on our side, He does not force His will upon us. He has given us free will to choose to serve Him or Satan.

In the following scripture, we are warned where our love and attention should be focused:

> Love not the world, neither the things that are in the world. If any man love the world, the love of the Father is not in him. For all that is in the world, the lust of the flesh, and the lust of the eyes, and the pride of life, is not of the Father, but is of the world.
>
> — 1 John 2:15-16

After we are saved, the forces of evil conspire to stop us from attaining our individual God-given purpose to the world, making us weak and preventing us from being effective in the witnessing of Christ. It is at this level that the focus of our enemy's engagement with us is to stop us from attaining the goals Christ has set for us. Here, we find the devil is working through the lusts of world, the flesh, and the pride of life. Now, the warfare becomes more focused and personal.

Beloved, think it not strange concerning the fiery trial which is to try you, as though some strange thing happened unto you: But rejoice, inasmuch as ye are partakers of Christ's sufferings; that, when his glory shall be revealed, ye may be glad also with exceeding joy.

— 1 Peter 4:12-13

The Bible tells us that the Holy Spirit within us is our proof and seal of redemption and where we will spend eternity. According to Ephesians 1:13 "In whom ye also trusted, after that ye heard the word of truth, the gospel of your salvation: in whom also after that ye believed, ye were sealed with that Holy Spirit of promise." This is crucial to the understanding of the believer. It is no longer an issue of salvation, once we have the Holy Spirit living within us. God has placed upon His believers a seal whereby we are recognized as God's beloved. The Holy Spirit is God's seal of approval upon us! He is our stamp of approval, granting us entry into eternity with God!

Chapter Twelve

The Ministry of Deliverance and Inner Healing

God desires that every believer would experience peace in their entire being, and this begins with our heart and mind being on one accord with the will of God. "And the peace of God, which passeth all understanding, shall keep your hearts and minds through Christ Jesus." — Philippians 4:7

The ministry of deliverance and inner healing is the supernatural transference of God's people from a place of oppression to a place of freedom or breakthrough. Whether it be evil demonic pressure, struggling with a particular sin, or a fiery trial, deliverance involves the hand of God severing things in the spirit realm and setting us free. Deliverance can happen in different ways, by the move of the Holy Spirit in an individual's situation,

Velma J. Colston Biggers

93

or God's people can experience corporate deliverance, together, all at once.

John 11:44 reads, "And he that was dead came forth, bound hand and foot with graveclothes: and his face was bound about with a napkin. Jesus saith unto them, Loose him, and let him go." It was in this passage of scripture that I first noticed the ministry of deliverance and inner healing. Here we have a man who was dead in every respect, and Jesus spoke life to his dead body. After reading this scripture, Ephesians 2:1 came to mind, "And you hath he quickened, who were dead in trespasses and sins." When we are born again, we are no longer dead in our trespasses and sins, but alive in Christ Jesus.

> Therefore we are buried with him by baptism into death: that like as Christ was raised up from the dead by the glory of the Father, even so we also should walk in newness of life.
>
> — Romans 6:4

Although we are now raised to a new life in Christ Jesus, it does not mean we automatically shed our grave clothes. That is part of the sanctification and the perfecting process, and it is the responsibility of each child of God, along with the church, to get rid of the grave clothes so we can live holy. Grave clothes are the clothes in which a dead person is buried. They represent habits and behaviors from our old life, prior to Christ.

Contrary to what some want to believe, we do not suddenly take off our old behaviors when we are born again. It involves a process. As we walk with God and our mind is conformed to the mind of Christ, we begin to think like Him and act like Him. We begin to take off old behaviors and put on new, that is, righteous behavior. If our grave clothes are not removed, they will keep us bound and gagged, actually imprisoned, by our own fleshly behaviors. Unfortunately, many Christians never take off their grave clothes and they end up living their entire lives in those smelly garments that represent the deadness and corruption of our old sin nature.

> And he gave some, apostles; and some, prophets; and some, evangelists; and some, pastors and teachers; For the perfecting of the saints, for the work of the ministry, for the edifying of the body of Christ: Till we all come in the unity of the faith, and of the knowledge of the Son of God, unto a perfect man, unto the measure of the stature of the fulness of Christ: That we henceforth be no more children, tossed to and fro, and carried about with every wind of doctrine, by the sleight of men, and cunning craftiness, whereby they lie in wait to deceive; But speaking the

truth in love, may grow up into him
in all things, which is the head, even
Christ:
— Ephesians 4:11-15.

The above passage of scripture gives us the
means to help discard our grave clothes. Jesus was
talking to the church in John 11:44 when He said,
"Loose him, and let him go!" He was telling the
church to help Lazarus remove his grave clothes.
When we are born again, we shed the things of the
old life to embrace and clothe ourselves with the
apparel of our new life in Christ. He has provided
through his finished work on the cross and his resurrection new clothing labeled "righteousness" and
"holiness." They are glorious, pure, and beautiful.
As we put on the mind of Christ, we become robed
in these new garments. "Therefore if any man be in
Christ, he is a new creature: old things are passed
away; behold, all things are become new." — 2 Corinthians 5:17

In Ephesians 4:12 and John 11:44, we find the
true purpose of the church. It is to prepare itself; the
bride for the bridegroom. The ministries of deliverance and inner healing are kingdom ministries,
whereby the oppressed are set free from demonic
power and influences. These ministries are part of
the sanctification process for the believer to bring
us closer to our potential in Christ. Sanctification
is the action of making or declaring something

Velma J. Colston Biggers

holy; it is the process of being purified or freed from sin. The process of sanctification requires deliberate action on our part because the believer must be willing to subject himself to the purifying process of God. The deliverance ministry deals primarily with the expelling of demons. However, the inner healing ministry, with the leading of the Holy Spirit, digs deep within our heart to destroy whatever bitter roots might be hiding, and prevents them from springing back to life.

As we minister to people, we often encounter candidates for deliverance who have pain deep within. Some do not even have an awareness of the pain or the source. However, when past memories surface, they will often expose emotions that we may not have been aware of. These emotions are often indicative of brokenness we need to deal with, and be healed from, so we can experience the liberty, joy, and peace in Christ. We are told to:

> Follow peace with all men, and holiness, without which no man shall see the Lord: Looking diligently lest any man fail of the grace of God; lest any root of bitterness springing up trouble you, and thereby many be defiled;
>
> — Hebrews 12:14-15

Exactly what is the root of bitterness? It is a mindset and emotion which is underground; it is hidden and camouflaged in the heart. Most people will not admit they are bitter; they will either deny it or disguise it. A bitter person is often hypersensitive, ungrateful, insincere, holds grudges, and has mood swings. Bitterness will affect you physically, emotionally, and spiritually because the fruit of bitterness is like an acid that destroys its container. God has to reveal it. We say, "I know my heart, I am not bitter." The truth is we don't know our heart. Jeremiah 17:9 tells us, "The heart is deceitful above all things, and desperately wicked: who can know it?

A deceitful heart cannot diagnose a deceitful heart. Bitterness is never right even when it seems justified because someone offends us. We need the Holy Spirit to help us rid our heart of bitterness. The Holy Spirit can identify it, expose it, and at our request, surgically remove it. That is just one of the reasons why we need the indwelling of the Holy Spirit. We need Him to help us to learn how to replace bitterness with peace. Hebrews 12:14 says, "Follow peace with all men, and holiness, without which no man shall see the Lord." Bitterness is very serious because it defiles us so we cannot move forward in God. Forgiveness is powerful because when we forgive, we set two people free — one of them is us!

What I have witnessed after over 30 years of being saved, is that most believers, at one time or

Velma J. Colston Biggers

another, need the ministry of deliverance and inner healing. Yet, this ministry is often shunned and disregarded mostly because the devil does not want us to know the power we possess in the authority of Jesus Christ. Too often, this ministry has been sensationalized and totally misunderstood, causing it to appear scary and demonic in nature when it is actually the opposite. It is the means to which Christ has given His Body to rid us of demonic influence. It is very important that we understand Satan hates this ministry, and he will fight to the bitter end to cause it to be rejected, so he can hold onto the captives. God has provided this ministry to dismantle the heavy burdens of oppression that the people of God do not realize are trying to destroy their lives. Certainly, God's people are destroyed for lack of knowledge!

Inner healing is the application of the Blood, the Cross, and the resurrected Life of our Lord Jesus Christ, to those stubborn areas of our heart that have not been redeemed. Through prayer, the Holy Spirit will lead and guide us into specific truths by prompting the right questions to unlock secrets of demonic strongholds that are key to the bondages in our lives. In doing so, He will lead us into the liberty that will produce freedom and growth in our lives as believers. Gods' intent is that deliverance and inner healing be available to every believer in the Body of Christ.

If leaders do not possess the skills of a deliverance minister, they should pray that God will give them the knowledge to minister deliverance to the flock He has given them to oversee. Sometimes God will lead them to a ministry that flows in this gifting and can help strengthen and counsel in this area. Leaders should never fear losing members to those better versed in the area of deliverance and inner healing. We need to look at it as an opportunity to learn and grow. The main concern should be the spiritual welfare of the people of God. God honors leaders who will look to Him to supply the needs of His people even if the source may be outside of that leader. The Lord has provided everything we need to mature the sons of God within the Body of Christ.

The Christian church is like a human body. It is one individual organism made up of many different parts that serve a wide variety of functions. 1 Corinthians 12:12, "For as the body is one, and hath many members, and all the members of that one body, being many, are one body: so also is Christ."

Contrary to what some believe, every individual church may not possess every spiritual gift needed for the growth and development of its' members. However, God has provided everything needed for the development of each member within the Body of Christ. Maybe your local church does not flow in the deliverance and inner healing ministry. However, God has given this ministry to be a blessing, and through prayer, He will direct your steps to a ministry that will lead you to freedom in this area.

Velma J. Colston Biggers

We must respect and value each other for the vital roles we serve in the Body of Christ, the church. As leaders we cannot allow our personal lack of knowledge to cause us to walk in fear and pride, but we should seek this knowledge of God, when necessary, through another ministry. We must pray that God will open the hearts of pastors and leaders to acknowledge the deliverance and inner healing ministries, as they are crucial for the advancement of the Body of Christ. Luke 11:9, "And I say unto you, Ask, and it shall be given you; seek, and ye shall find; knock, and it shall be opened unto you." God has made provision for all the needs of His people.

Every problem we experience in this life is not caused by demons. While Satan has been the cause of more people running into the arms of Christ than anything else, he is a created being with a purpose and employed by God. God has placed limitations on what Satan can do and he is not the source of all our problems. Some of our problems are related to personal decisions made, relationship issues, family matters, financial decisions, etc. The point is, we need the ability to discern when our problem is simply a part of life or when there may be an evil supernatural source working behind it.

Conclusion

Brothers and Sisters, there is an invisible war raging all around us. It is a war between the Kingdom of Light and the Kingdom of Darkness — good versus evil competing for the souls of men. In this war, we do not fight against flesh and blood. According to Ephesians 6:12, our war is "...against principalities, against powers, against the rulers of the darkness of this world, and against spiritual wickedness in high places."

The arena we battle in is in the spirit, and the weapons of our warfare are not weapons of this world but are spiritual weapons of mass destruction through our Lord and Savior Jesus Christ, who has already given us the victory. We are designed and equipped to take charge in the earth and stand against our demonic enemy, so that we nor our families become casualties of *The Invisible War*!

My hope is that this book will encourage God's people to see our calling from Our Heavenly

Father's perspective. I pray we will stand up to the demonic forces that, for so long, have engaged in war against us and laughed at our futile attempts to fight with the weapons of men and not the weapons God has provided for us.

When we dress in the full armor of God and release the Word of God in faith, it will hit the target and accomplish what it is designed to do. We will see the fulfillment of "...if God be for us, who can be against us?" — Romans 8:31

Engaging in spiritual warfare is not meant to draw unwarranted attention to what the devil is doing. Its purpose is to focus on God and pay attention to what *He* is doing and represent *Him* with our absolute best!

I pray we will seek God with repentant hearts, so our families will be free from generational curses and every demonic stronghold purposed to stop us from walking in our divine destiny. May the Holy Spirit reveal the hidden things of the spirit and lead us and guide us into all truth. Let us stand up against the powers of darkness and declare the Kingdom of God has come! We, the sons of God, must preach and demonstrate His great commission as He commanded in Mark 16:15-18;

> *And he said unto them, Go ye into all the world, and preach the gospel to every creature. He that believeth and is baptized shall be saved; but he that believeth not shall be damned.*

And these signs shall follow them that believe; In my name shall they cast out devils; they shall speak with new tongues; They shall take up serpents; and if they drink any deadly thing, it shall not hurt them; they shall lay hands on the sick, and they shall recover.

My sincere desire is that *The Invisible War: A Glimpse Into Spiritual Warfare* will challenge the way we think about who we are as Christians and what God has commissioned us to do. May we pray and seek the face of God, allowing Him to use us as His instruments in the earth, facilitating His plan for the salvation of all men.

Signs You May Be Under Spiritual Attack

Spiritual Warfare is an everyday occurrence for believers and unbelievers alike. I have listed below some signs that may alert us to spiritual warfare being engaged against our personal lives and ministry. We should pray and guard ourselves in the areas of our strengths, weaknesses, and influence. These attacks are specifically designed, timed, and personalized for each person.

1. <u>Severe discouragement and confusion</u>. You feel defeated and depressed. Things seem hopeless, overwhelming, and burdensome. You find yourself stressed and struggling with a loss of vision and a lack of peace. You may feel like giving up. You may experience disorientation, withdrawal, and despair, which can lead to defeat.

2. <u>Loss of vision and spiritual desire</u>. You experience difficulty praying, being connected to other Christians, and maintaining the vision for your ministry.

3. <u>Physical fatigue and/or malaise</u>. You feel drained, lacking energy, no motivation.

4. <u>Negative tapes playing, disturbing thought life</u>. You may be wrestling with anxiety, fear, or worrisome thoughts. The enemy attacks your mind, and the mind is the battlefield.

5. <u>Thoughts about going back to your old lifestyle and habits</u>. You may be tempted to "turn back." The enemy will try to tempt you with the things you have been delivered from.

6. <u>Old emotional wounds from the past resurfaced</u>. You believed you had dealt with that area of pain in your life, only to find it is cropping up again. The enemy can use hurtful memories to hinder you in your walk with God.

7. <u>Battling with feelings of guilt, condemnation, and shame</u>. You are still feeling shameful about the sins of your past. The enemy is an accuser. He wants you to feel that you are not good enough, you have not done enough, and you are not forgiven.

8. <u>Feelings of rejection, belonging and loneliness</u>. You feel no one accepts you and you do not know where you belong, if

anywhere. The enemy loves to isolate believers from the power found in fellowship.

9. <u>Confusion over what you believe</u>. You wonder if Jesus is *really* the only way. The enemy tries to sow messages that are contrary to the words God has spoken or has revealed in the Bible. Confusion can also be apparent in relationships where communication becomes distorted, perverted, and misrepresented.

10. <u>Extreme temptation to sin</u>. You are struggling with sinful thoughts and desires. Temptation originates with our own weakness and ungodly desires, but the enemy can use situations and people around us to apply extreme or sudden pressure on us in these areas.

> Let no man say when he is tempted, I am tempted of God: for God cannot be tempted with evil, neither tempteth he any man: But every man is tempted, when he is drawn away of his own lust, and enticed. Then when lust hath conceived, it bringeth forth sin: and sin, when it is finished, bringeth forth death.
>
> — James 1:13-15

11. <u>Atmosphere of pressure or oppression</u>. You feel a sense of heaviness. The enemy seeks to overwhelm you.

12. <u>Crippling condemnation that is unclear</u>. You feel condemned. It is different from the Holy Spirit's conviction; this feeling comes with no rhyme or reason regarding what the condemnation is all about.

13. <u>Intimidation and fear</u>. You feel as if *you can't*. This is especially so when fear is pressuring you to stop moving in the direction of God's revealed will for your life, or that of your family, ministry, or church.

14. <u>Evil memory recall</u>. You feel as if a reel is repeatedly playing your past sinful events, in order to bring up false guilt and shame. Your sins have already been covered by the Blood of Jesus Christ.

If you find yourself under spiritual attack...

- Do not give in to fear!
- Take arms with the Word of God.
- Gird up! Pray with the Word of God!

There is nothing more frightening to Satan than a believer who is fully equipped with spiritual armor!

Velma J. Colston Biggers

Meditation and Warfare Scriptures

Scriptures to Encourage You During Spiritual
Attack

King James Version

Deuteronomy 28:7

> The Lord shall cause thine enemies that
> rise up against thee to be smitten before thy
> face: they shall come out against thee one
> way, and flee before thee seven ways.

Isaiah 54:17

> No weapon that is formed against thee shall
> prosper; and every tongue that shall rise
> against thee in judgment thou shalt con-
> demn. This is the heritage of the servants of

the Lord, and their righteousness is of me, saith the Lord.

Zech. 4:6

Then he answered and spake unto me, saying, This is the word of the Lord unto Zerubbabel, saying, Not by might, nor by power, but by my spirit, saith the Lord of hosts.

Matthew 18:18-20

[18]Verily I say unto you, Whatsoever ye shall bind on earth shall be bound in heaven: and whatsoever ye shall loose on earth shall be loosed in heaven. [19]Again I say unto you, That if two of you shall agree on earth as touching any thing that they shall ask, it shall be done for them of my Father which is in heaven. [20]For where two or three are gathered together in my name, there am I in the midst of them.

Luke 1:37

For with God nothing shall be impossible.

Luke 10:19

Behold, I give unto you power to tread on serpents and scorpions, and over all the power of the enemy: and nothing shall by any means hurt you.

Romans 8:37

> Nay, in all these things we are more than conquerors through him that loved us.

2 Corinthians 10:3-5

> [3]For though we walk in the flesh, we do not war after the flesh: [4](For the weapons of our warfare are not carnal, but mighty through God to the pulling down of strong holds;) [5]Casting down imaginations, and every high thing that exalteth itself against the knowledge of God, and bringing into captivity every thought to the obedience of Christ;

Ephesians 6:10-13

> [10]Finally, my brethren, be strong in the Lord, and in the power of his might. [11]Put on the whole armour of God, that ye may be able to stand against the wiles of the devil. [12]For we wrestle not against flesh and blood, but against principalities, against powers, against the rulers of the darkness of this world, against spiritual wickedness in high places. [13]Wherefore take unto you the whole armour of God, that ye may be able to withstand in the evil day, and having done all, to stand.

James 4:7-8

> [7]Submit yourselves therefore to God. Resist the devil, and he will flee from you. [8]Draw nigh to God, and he will draw nigh to you. Cleanse your hands, ye sinners; and purify your hearts, ye double minded.

John 8:32

> And ye shall know the truth, and the truth shall make you free.

John 10:10

> The thief cometh not, but for to steal, and to kill, and to destroy: I am come that they might have life, and that they might have it more abundantly.

2 Timothy 1:7

> For God hath not given us the spirit of fear; but of power, and of love, and of a sound mind.

1 Peter 5:8-9

> [8]Be sober, be vigilant; because your adversary the devil, as a roaring lion, walketh about, seeking whom he may devour: [9]Whom resist stedfast in the faith, knowing that the same afflictions are accomplished in your brethren that are in the world.

Velma J. Colston Biggers

1 John 4:4

> Ye are of God, little children, and have over-come them: because greater is he that is in you, than he that is in the world.

1 John 5:4-5

> [4]For whatsoever is born of God overcometh the world: and this is the victory that over-cometh the world, even our faith. [5]Who is he that overcometh the world, but he that believeth that Jesus is the Son of God?

Revelation 12:11

> And they overcame him by the blood of the Lamb, and by the word of their testimony; and they loved not their lives unto the death.

Revelation 20:10

> And the devil that deceived them was cast into the lake of fire and brimstone, where the beast and the false prophet are, and shall be tormented day and night for ever and ever.

Resources

I found these resources to be helpful in my research and reflection. You may find them helpful as well.

Behind Enemy Lines .... Charles H, Kraft, Tom White, Ed Murphy & Others, Servant Publications

Deliverance and Spiritual
Warfare Manual .... John Eckhardt, Charisma House

Evicting Demonic Squatters &
Breaking Bondages .... Noel and Phyl Gibson, Freedom in Christ Ministries Trust

Generational Curses and the
Biblical Remedies .... Pastor Ikechukwu
Chinedum

Marked For God's Commanded
Blessing! .... Dr. Morris Cerullo,
Morris Cerullo
World Evangelism

The Believers Guide to
Spiritual Warfare .... Thomas B.
White, Servant
Publications

The Bondage Breaker .... Neil T. Anderson,
Harvest House
Publishers

The Holy Bible... (King James Ver-
sion,
New International
Version)

The Kingdom of God
Suffers Violence .... John Elliot Wil-
liams,
CreateSpace Inde-
pendent
Publishing
Platform

References

Britannica, T. Editors of Encyclopaedia. "devil." *Encyclopedia Britannica*, August 22, 2022. https://www.britannica.com/topic/devil.

Merriam-Webster.com Dictionary, s.v. "divination," accessed August 28, 2022.
https://www.merriam-webster.com/dictionary/divination.

Merriam-Webster.com Dictionary, s.v. "knowledge," accessed August 28, 2022.
https://www.merriam-webster.com/dictionary/knowledge.

Wikipedia. 2021. "Ignorantia juris non excusat. Last modified August 18, 2022.
https://en.wikipedia.org/wiki/Ignorantia_juris_non_excusat

Wikipedia. 2022. "Divination." Last modified August 6, 2022.
https://en.wikipedia.org/wiki/Divination

About the Author

Velma J. Colston Biggers is an ordained minister of the Gospel of the Lord Jesus Christ. She is the founder of BELIEVE AGAIN WORLD WIDE MINISTRIES a ministry that hosts conferences and events that specialize in the healing, building and maturing of the sons and daughters of God. CHOSEN: Women of Influence, a ministry of women who share a common passion for the truth of the Gospel to be preached. They are willing to be examples of holiness, standing for one thing.... God's truth. Their desire is to mature in the Word of God.

These ministries are designed to provide an atmosphere for spiritual impartation and growth and are dedicated to the broken and the bruised. Velma hosted the radio show, *Believe Again* at Worship Center Radio and *Believe Again Radio Program* on WCHB.

While Velma does not claim to be an expert in the area of deliverance and inner healing, she has several years of on-the-job training and counseling experience in the capacities of Assistant Pastor and Associate Pastor. Much of the information contained in this book is a result of that experience. Velma has been blessed to witness amazing transformation in the lives of people who have been delivered from demonic oppression. Her passion is to see the people of God walking in the freedom and power of God's authority and truth!

Made in the USA
Middletown, DE
22 October 2023